PAKISTAN
A POLITICAL HISTORY OF STATE

ZULFIQAR SHAH

AN ISM PUBLICATION

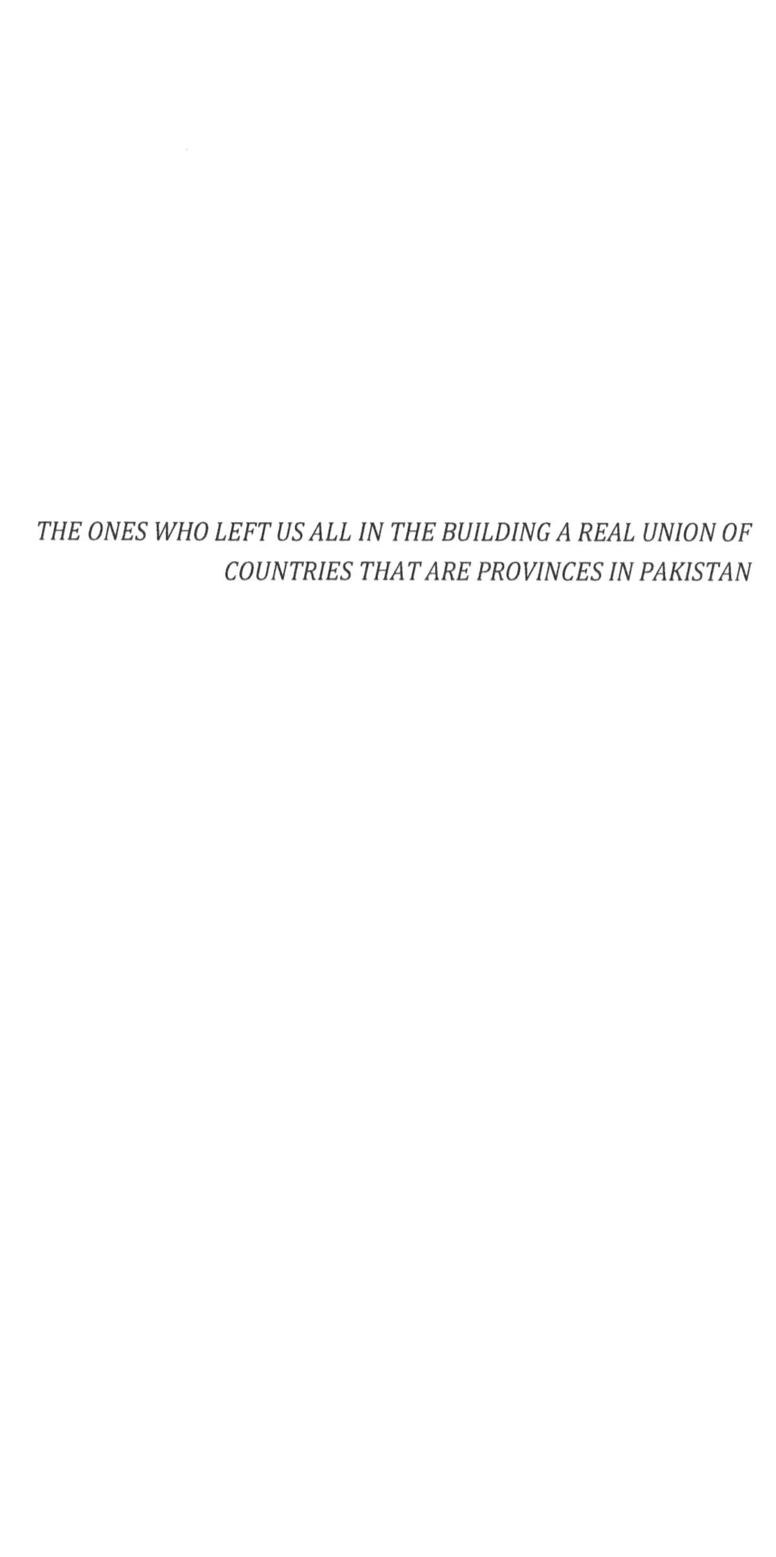

*THE ONES WHO LEFT US ALL IN THE BUILDING A REAL UNION OF
COUNTRIES THAT ARE PROVINCES IN PAKISTAN*

THE level of instability, peace, and human insecurity Pakistan undergoes since at least last decade falls under the category of state failure. It has started exhibiting the symptoms and indicators of state failure. An academic inquiry is required to understand the foundations as well as contemporary magnitude of the crisis. According to Jackson[1], a state is said to be failed if it cannot maintain the minimum civil conditions like peace, order, and security. The 'inability to govern' also is an important indicator for the state failure, in which the states fail to meet the fundamental needs of the citizens. The US Congress Commission on Weak States and US National Security[2] further elaborates the three-fold parameters for the failed state, which include inability to ensure security, meeting the basic needs of the population and maintaining state legitimacy.

In post cold-war era, rise in the violent conflicts around the globe has been evident. In some parts of the third world, enduring warfare and civil conflicts resulted into the "total breakdown of legitimate authority, affecting not just states, but entire regions,"[3] resulting into the fall, disintegration and decay of the states, which has opened up a new debate in the global politics.

Nations on the globe are concerned about the risks posed by the failed states, due to which the issues like proliferation of Weapons of Mass Destruction (WMD) and of ballistic missiles have attained centrality. A nuclear war between major powers is unlikely to happen from the global security perspective; however, it is feared that some nuclear capable 'rogue states', due their state fragility and anarchy, possibly offend the opponents. Besides, the non-proliferation of state-actors and assumed *nuclearizition* of non-state actors has raised the global security concerns. In fact, "failed states, rogue states, belligerent and powerful non-state actors seems to have taken hold of world politics."[4] In this alarming context of global insecurity, it is therefore niche to analyze nuclear capable Pakistan, which gradually is inching towards chaos and anarchy due to state failure.

Genesis of Pakistan

Pakistan emerged on the world map in 1947 as a federation of pre-British occupation sovereign countries of Sindh, Balochistan and Punjab as well as some ethno-linguistic Pashtu parts of Afghanistan that were situated on the both sides of river Indus. It came into being due to the politics of communal dissent by the religious minority Muslims in Indian Subcontinent during the British colonial rule. The primary concept of Pakistan got birth naively during 1940, when a separate Union for South

Asian Muslims was demanded comprising of "sovereign and autonomous states of Sindh, Punjab, NWFP, Balochistan and East Bengal."[5] This was, in fact, a reaction to the British India Act (the constitution) of 1935, which created a highly centralized political system.[6] An ideological justification and rational was provided for the creation of the new country a few years before its creation, which is called 'two-nation theory' based on so-called Hindu and Muslim nationhood within the united India. However, no political doctrine or theoretical treatise of so-called two-nation theory has ever existed in the political discourse of Indian Subcontinent.

In early twentieth century, the Indian National Congress (INC) – a secular political party, converted itself into a large and cohesive non-violent popular political movement in colonial India. After a decade, All India Muslim League (AIML) was founded clubbing together the Muslim aristocracy **the East Bengal** of United Provinces (UP) and Central Provinces (CP) of the north and central India, where Muslims were minority among the Hindus majority. The AIML's aristocrat leadership from Muslim minority provinces was core demander of Muslim rights. **AIML movement by the Muslim majority provinces in British Empire called India consisting Sindh, Punjab, and East Bengal incepted Pakistan movement after 1940.** Bidding farewell to their colonial rule in 1947, British finally endorsed the two-nation theory and divided India into two independent states: the provinces with a Muslim majority population formed Pakistan, the rest were the Union of India. At the time of Indian partition, Balochistan was not part of Pakistan. Qalat Khanate (Balochi speaking Balochistan) was an independent sovereign state with a bicameral parliament, cabinet and a head of the state. Pakistan Army invaded Balochistan in 1948.[7] The only cementing force between the provinces of newly formed Pakistan was the Indus Civilization but unfortunately, the *two-nations* theory based on religious nationhood was a negation of the Indus Civilization.

Pakistani scholar Hamza Alavi, himself a Indian partition refugee, writes, "Pakistan was not just an ideological state; it was a 'migrant state' as well."[8] Partition of India was not merely a geographical division of Indian Subcontinent but also a division of resources including the human resources for running the state affairs. The division of civil and military bureaucracy was also part of the Partition Plan. This turned the newly formed state into an ethnically exclusive state apparatus. Non-indigenous to newly formed country, Urdu speaking Muslim from UP and CP regions of undivided India formed newly born Pakistan's civil bureaucracy and ethnic Punjabi dominated military undertook the security responsibility of the country. This created a new situation where state remained oddly distant from society and in many instances against the will of the indigenous majority. Thus, "a dualism of state and society was established.[9]"

Socio-political fabric
During the partition, West Pakistan (now Pakistan) was a rural society with strong feudal background in comparison with the East Pakistan (now Bangladesh) that was comparatively urbanized with a vibrant, dynamic, and literate middle class. The ethnic Punjabi dominated army of the newly formed Pakistan inherited British legacy and hence collaborated with the landed aristocracy as well as corrupt civil bureaucracy to attain major role in the state field in a bid to serve the interests of Punjab.

The Britain's strategy of ruling colonial India through local power brokers and middlemen was adopted by AIML leadership, which itself was immigrant in the newly formed Pakistan. Besides, majority of AIML leadership was hailing from Ganga-Jamuna civilization belt of northern India, who now attained the role of vanguard in Indus-Sarswati civilization centre of the South-western India (Pakistan). This cultural difference was also at the helm many wrongdoings in the foundations of the Pakistani state building.

In fact, Pakistan neither was demanded by any of the federating state of the undivided India nor was it a public demand of the Muslim majority states. In the 1946 Indian elections, AIML could not won majority in Punjab, NWFP (now Khyber Pakhtunkhuwa) and East Bengal (now Bangladesh), which was certainly a referendum against partition of India or carving a new country out of India. In 1946, the AIML leadership and parliamentarians from Sindh who legislated for Pakistan in 1943 in Sindh Legislative Assembly became arch opponents of Pakistan's creation as well as communal politics of AIML. Sindh Legislative Assembly voted for Pakistan only because the INC and Hindu population of Sindh opposed the separation of Sindh from Bombay Presidency in 1930s, meanwhile AIML supported the demand mostly because Mohammad Ali Jinnah was an ethnic Sindhi. In 1843, British invaded Sindh as a sovereign country, and later on annexed it with Bombay in 1850s. The indigenous population in Muslim majority states of India did not buy the idea of Pakistan, as they were historically not only secular but also independent countries of their times.

Ethnic, linguistic, class and economic issues, not the religious ones, are the real political dynamic of contemporary Pakistan. Religious parties and their terrorist outfits derived power through the patronage of the Pakistani establishment during the military regime of General Zia, which were further strengthened later on. Pakistani security establishment has historically been articulating the religious sentiments as a counter balance to the liberal and secular essence of the indigenous societies in Pakistan on the rotten lines of pre-Indian partition AIML. This has further strengthened the gradual disintegration of Pakistan because it has failed so far in building a Pakistan society and nation as such. Instead, Sindhi, Pashtun, Balochi, Punjabi, Siraiki, Hindko and Baltistani societies and ethnic-nationhood still has extensively groomed. Meanwhile, Pakistan's economy continuously exhibits the downtrend, with continuously reducing the chances of its recovery and self-reliance. The political deinstitutionalization, militarization, *Punjabization*, corruption, bad governance, poor education, weak political parties, domestic disorder, and a drowning economy are the major threats to the survival of Pakistan.

Chemistry of state building

Max Weber[10] terms the state a political community that is capable to control the means of the legitimate use of physical violence for maintenance of peace, order, and security. In the context of Weber's interpretation, it the analysis of internal or external, ethnic and / or classes, and other social segments for their role in process of state building in Pakistan and its transformation through different phases reveals the factors leading state failure of Pakistan, in which the country has started sharing its legitimacy over the use of violence with numerous non-state actors.

Pakistani state since its embryos has been a Punjabi-cum-Urdu led organism of human resources. "Along with the hegemony of the landowning and industrial elites, the bureaucratic apparatus of the Pakistani state was mainly controlled by the Punjabis."[11] The Punjabi domination is continuation of pre-independence colonial legacy, hence; provide bases for the politico-economic privileges of one ethnic group over the others. British patronized ethnic Punjabis in the military who subsequently supported their colonial rule as well as fought on their side during the Second World War on several war fronts.

Since Punjab constituted demographic majority of the West Pakistan, which formed beyond three quarters of the Pakistan army before Pakistan's break-up in 1971, "the bloodshed at the partition had a strong effect on army and state in Pakistan."[12] Therefore, to greater extent, Pakistan – India conflict in its origin is a conflict between West Punjab (Indian Refugees) and India. Both countries have fought four wars over Kashmir; hence, India has become a corner stone in the security doctrine of the state and military in Pakistan.

Along with partition riots as well as "initial phase of armed state-building"[13], Pakistan's inclusion into cold war in 1954 also left its impacts on the state building. The flow of military aid by US further strengthened the military's development in comparison with the society and civil actors, which consequently gave Pakistani military an edge over the civilians in the process of state building. "Due to the US assistance, Pakistan Army grew in size, morale, and skills."[14] "Educational standards (of the military elite class) became higher than civilian(s)."[15] "Pakistan's top military officials gained exclusive access to the decision makers in Washington [...] Soon military became an integral part of (West-) Pakistan's ruling alliance, which included the refugee civil bureaucracy and the immigrant bourgeoisie as well."[16] The country has witnessed four military rules so far in the sixty-five years. According to Hamza Alvi[17], Pakistan's armed forces and their "overdeveloped state" tried to accommodate pressure arising from newly mobilized social forces (during Z. A. Bhutto period) and a more hostile international environment. Boris Wilke[18] writes that they did succeed only at the expense of the coherency, strength, and autonomy of both the armed forces and the state apparatus as a whole.

According the available research work, Pakistani state has undergone three phases of transformation -- Migrant, Overdeveloped and Garrison State. However, due to the changing socio-political and strategic realities after 9/11, it has steadily undergone the metabolism and transformation of fourth and fifth phases altogether of being 'Civilly-Militarized State' and Fragile-Statehood. At the time of partition, it was a Migrant state, which gradually transformed into an 'over developed state'; later on transformed into 'garrison state' and finally has culminated into civilly militarized as well as fragile-state.

(a)   'Migrant State'

Boris Wilke[19] terms the early partition statehood of Pakistan as a 'Migrant State.' It was not only led by the migrant bureaucracy but also through the migrant AIML leadership as well as military fraternity. 'Pakistan idea' supporters were concentrated largely in UP and CP of undivided India and belonged to the urbanized Muslim aristocracy and city dwelling poor. During and after partition, they migrated to the Muslim majority provinces, which became Pakistan in 1947. On the other hand, the indigenous population of the Muslim majority states was mostly having an urbanized elite and middle class of Hindu and Sikh besides urban poor, whereas Muslims were almost landed aristocracy and peasantry with lower literacy ratio.

Although migrations were not part of partition plan but the violence due to division of India led Hindus and Sikhs from Punjab in 1947 and from Sindh in 1948 to migrate towards India; meanwhile Punjabi and Urdu-speaking Muslims took refuge in newly formed Pakistan. This created a socio-economic makeshift and upheaval in Punjab, Sindh, and East Bengal. The refugees of ethnic Punjabi origin from India settled in Punjab and the Urdu lingual refugees settled in Sindh. They not only acquired houses, agriculture land, and other assets outgoing Hindu and Sikh but also got an exclusive space in the civil and military bureaucracy as well as governance of the newly formed state. The partition influx caused demographic catastrophe in Sindh with the outflow of Hindus and influx of Urdu speaking Muslims. The process had an irregular pattern. Hindus never decided to quit Sindh but due to violence unleashed by refugee Muslims, now identifying themselves *Muhajirs*, they left Sindh declining the appeals by Sindh Government for not leaving their ancestral land.

Such a demographic divergence of Sindh in early period of Pakistan has left its ever-lasting impacts on the society, polity, and economy of the province. According to Sara Ansari[20], the exodus of Hindus from Sindh made available vast tracts of land, residential property and other local commercial enterprises. For instance, the rural Waderas (chieftains) seized 800,000 acres out of the 1,345,000 acreage abandoned by Hindus, although mostly the refugees from India obtained the urban properties, as well as rural estate properties including houses, farms, and irrigative lands.

The increasing pressure of refugees forced Pakistan government to handover evacuee property to them on the basis of claims regarding their left over property in India; however many of the claims for evacuee property by the refugees were either false or exaggerated. According to Sara Ansari[21], just five per cent of Sindh's inhabitants owned 95 per cent of agricultural land, leaving 2.6 million landless peasants in a pitiable state. While the *Muhajir* and Sindhi politicians engaged in a power struggle, the peasants were largely left on their own. She writes that the institutionalization of the urban refugee population through educational, media, civic and commercial forums afforded them better opportunities for lobbying, which extended to their assumption of an air of victimhood, derived from the sacrifices that they had rendered to come to Pakistan.

Muhajir and Punjabi elite were allies in the exploitation of East Pakistan and rest ethnicities in West Pakistan. Due to their fear of numerical majority of Bengalis, they imposed war over them in 1971. "Urdu and a centralized system of government were deemed synonymous with Pakistani nationhood and against a background of economic and political stalemate, Pakistan's already weak political culture began to see more and more interference from the civil and military wings of the bureaucracy."[22]

Notwithstanding, the political landscape was dominated by the powerful provincial and rural actors. Taking this in the context, the first Prime Minister of Pakistan Liaqat Ali Khan, who himself migrated from Muslim minority areas of India, settled north and central Indian refugees (Muhajirs) in Karachi, Hyderabad and Sukkur cities of Sindh in a bid to create electoral constituencies for the migrant AIML leadership in future. In one of his highly controversial speech, he said that the civilization of Sindh is nothing but a culture of the donkey pullers and camel herders.[23] In contemporary politics of Pakistan Mutahida Qomi Movement (MQM) is representing these Urdu speaking refugees' community to maintain the privileges they attained during partition at the cost of indigenous rural inhabitance. Besides, the first or the second generation of these Urdu speaking and Punjabi refugees is the dominant majority within civil and military bureaucracy ad well as judiciary. Majority of the military generals of the country's mighty army also belong to the first or the second generations of these refugees. It would be correct to say that politics of statecraft in Pakistan even today is the result of ethnic chemistry of the Pakistani statehood, in which Sindhi, Baloch and Pashtun ethnicities, women, religious minorities and certain schools of thought find no space.

In this 'migrant state' phase, the state was shaped by the migrant Muslims from north and central India. They took hold of state building process though their British civil service legacy, maintained gap between state and society and formed the political system that suited them best. The *Muhajirs* had no interest in democracy in which majority indigenous rural population led by the landed aristocracy would have taken the hold of state affairs. "As a class of traders, industrialists and civil servants, the *Muhajirs* needed a functioning state apparatus, which may have maintained the monopoly of the legitimate use of violence in their interests and give themselves some degree of predictability to social and economic life."[24] Lacking a political and demographic strength, they made collaboration with Punjab leadership, who represented majority of West Pakistan's population and was dominating the army. Hence, democracy was set aside at the very beginning of the country.

(b) 'Overdeveloped State'

Pakistan army since beginning was Punjabi dominated, with a fair higher number of ethnic Pashtun and Urdu speaking refugees with proportion to their populace. The intrusion of military in the political governance of the country, though joint collaboration of *Muhajir* civil bureaucracy and Punjabi military, transformed Pakistan from 'migrant state' into the 'overdeveloped state'. An overdeveloped state is the unevenly higher-level development of state vis-à-vis society, which was reached at in Pakistan when military developed its corporate interest as well as took hold of political governance by imposing military rule. "Democracy was held in abeyance. Vital and far-reaching decisions, such as the US Pakistan military alliance and economic policy strategy, had been taken by top bureaucrats (and military officers)."[25]

(c) Garrison State

According to Ayesha Jalal, defence matters had guided Pakistan's state-formation process since the beginning. "Defence spending not just posed a tremendous financial burden on Pakistan's 'state of martial law', accounting for the largest part of the budget for decades, more importantly, the underlying motives for state growth in general have been dictated by the necessity to expand the defence budget, in order to match the Indian military capacity."[26] She says that a "political economy of defence" provides the basis for Pakistan's superstructure having much plausibility.[27] The emergence of conflict over Kashmir, collaboration between Punjabi military and Urdu bureaucracy, and imprints of partition riots put the foundations of a 'garrison state' from the beginning that further strengthened after the transformation into the 'overdeveloped state'. The first military takeover in 1958 had been a move to further strengthen Punjab's dominancy and suppress East Pakistan, which eventually became Bangladesh after a brutal military operation and freedom war of 1971 as soon as Punjab dishonoured the electoral majority of East Pakistan based Awami League.

Pakistan lost 1971 war at ideological, internal (East Pakistan) and external (India) fronts. It primarily disproved 'two-nation' doctrine foundations of Pakistan, which were based on religion-nationhood because East Pakistan won sovereignty on the ethnic-nationalism of Bengalis. The defeat provided an agency to civilians in Pakistan to regain their lost powers of state-field. It was an exception in Pakistan's history, which never came again until the murder of Benazir Bhutto in 2007. Moreover, there was a chance to break the military's hegemony, which ultimately meant minimizing influence of ethnic Punjabi and lingual Urdu community and creating positive spaces for indigenous Sindhi, Baloch, Pashtun and Siraiki people within the state-fold. "(Zulfikar Ali) Bhutto favoured a much more active role of the state in relation to society and to its subjects.[28]" He also safeguarded feudal lords' interests by nationalizing industries of the country. Bhutto's biggest mistake was his half-hearted move for keeping military out of political realm and thereby out of power. Bhutto's silence over the brutal military suppression of the labour unrest in Karachi and provincial autonomy movement in Balochistan was a debacle. He also unnecessarily accepted the pressure of *Jamait-e-Islami* and other right wing parties for converting Pakistan constitutionally into an Islamic Republic that did not recognize Muslim-hood of Hamada community. Balochistan suppression escalated a civil war from 1973 to 1977. Bhutto, again, had to deploy the army. Thus, the "war-making brought the army back to state-making."[29] After at least four decades, President Asif Ali Zardari kept similar silence in 2011 over the murder of Salman Taseer, and was unable to resolve Balochistan conflict or end military operation.

Pakistan also violated the grammar of federalism in 1971 by dishonouring the vote of Bengal through which Awami League won majority in the parliament; however, the genesis of Bengali secessionism were already rooted in the two decades long exploitation of Bengal by the Punjabi-Urdu led establishment. After dismemberment of Pakistan, it was mandatory according to the federalism norms to elect a constitutional assembly for agreeing upon the new social contract between federating states; however, instead of electing a constitutional assembly, the remaining parliament of Pakistan formed the new constitution in 1973. Thus, the civil forces further provided space to military establishment and dominating Punjabi-Urdu ethnic groups for extensively militarizing remaining Pakistan.

Bhutto's government was toppled through a military coup d'état by military chief General Zia ul-Haq. Pakistan witnessed a far-reaching deteriorated social metabolism and state transformation under Zia regime. In this period, Pakistan created US sponsored *Jihadis* against USSR in Afghanistan that ultimately left disastrous impacts on Pakistan state and the society in long run. The entire security regime of the country was indoctrinated with *Salafiism* through advocating radicalization of Islam; which caused religious extremist groups actions in Pakistan, Afghanistan, and Indian Kashmir. Opiate and AK 47 jointly intruded Pakistan society. The religious extremism, political violence, and terrorism in today's Pakistan have foundations in the internal and foreign policies of General Zia era, which yet are being continued, however with entirely different outlook. During this, the intelligence agencies assumed manipulative role in almost all major realms of Pakistan, with focused infiltration in the political organism and process of the country.

(d) Civilly- militarized state

The political terms - Left and Right wings- of the ideological identification are replaced now in Pakistan with the new terms of 'military in the civilian' and 'civilian of the military' due to extensive militarization state field and society especially through the human engineering.

Being an all-time military republic, statecraft in Pakistan has always tried to fragment, divert, and pervert social ethos, cultural composition, and political discourse. Fanaticism, radical *Islamisation*, tribal fiefdoms, feudalism, ethnic chauvinism, and the fascism of Punjabis and *Muhajirs*, the chronic ailments of Pakistan, are an ultimate outcome of militarization and *Punjabization* of state and society. It has resulted from the divide-and-rule policy of the military establishment, which preferred unitary governance, non-substantive democracy and the ethno-sectarian monotony and monopoly of the state apparatus. [30]

Social and state fragmentation in Pakistan today is the ultimate consequence of decades' long hold of military over state affairs, which also necessarily safeguarded and furthered the interests of privileged ethnic groups, classes and militarized civilians that have emerged in Pakistan as a separate social entity. It has led Pakistan to the militarization of society and civil spaces in general.

Prioritizing militaristic security over the development paradigm, life quality, and socio-economic growth of the people down trended especially in Sindh, Balochistan and Khyber Pakhtunkhuwa provinces. Pakistan has now turned into a security state, where an unwritten constitution reins everything. The privileged ethnic groups like Punjabis and Urdu, and Islamic schools of thought like *Salafism* and *Devband* as considered as core patriotic demography, and entertain influence in the state affairs including development planning, internal and external security, and policy development perspective. The unending conflicts along with Pakistan's India and Afghan borders as well as the phenomena of Talibanisation are deeply rooted in it.

The hidden strings of conflict within the mighty security establishment of Pakistan are usually termed a 'proxy conflict between the hawks and doves', and such an antagonism has most of the time led country towards military rules in past and virtual coups these days. Knowing that military rule has no opportunity in future, they started supporting judiciary as proxy state pillar on behalf of the military. Therefore, "Khakis in Pakistan are the faultiness at the epicentre of judicial activism. The standoff between the two pillars of the republic is a sign and omen of undergoing a transformation simultaneously with a severe state crisis causing frictions outer layers of the governance."[31]

If defined in the précised terms, the history of Pakistan is the history of antagonism between Punjab led military in association with civilly militarized class and the civilians of the rest ethnicities. In broader terms, Punjabi-Urdu dominated military and their civilly militarized civil bureaucracy as well as politicians have been antagonistic towards Sindhi, Baloch and Pashtun, which are excluded the deeper state-field. Benazir Bhutto and Nawaz Sharif both have mentioned many a times about this, particularly in the context of election rigging. Although the civil-military relations in Pakistan have been at odds since long, however the current nature of the relations is two-decade-old phenomena. "On April 20, 1994 the then Interior Minister Nasrullah Babar raised an issue in the parliament of illegal disbursement of $6.5 million in 1990 to the fundamentalist and military cronies by the state owned Mehran Bank chief Yunus Habib. He was detained for the fraud on March 24, 1994. In 1997, Asghar Khan, a former chief of the Pakistan Air Force, filed a Supreme Court petition challenging the legality of the drawn money and its distribution."[32] It took a highly patchy route for the Supreme Court of

Pakistan, which after many years gave a decision that does not punish anyone.

"According to analysts of Pakistan's security profile, it was in 1950 when the first Prime Minister of the country Liaqat Ali Khan instructed the formation of the first ever security dogwatch immediately after the Pakistan-India war in October 1948 over Kashmir. The intrusion of security regime in the civilian domain of Pakistan began in 1955 when Major General (retired) Iskander Mirza became Governor General of the country, which was followed by Army Chief General Ayub Khan's take over on October 27, 1958. It was under Ayub Khan when country's security institutions started manipulating elections during the presidential election of 1964, in which Fatima Jinnah, leader of the Muslim League and sister of Jinnah, lost against the General." [33]

Pakistan- India war of 1965 created the new security challenges for Pakistan because Pakistan Army withdrew battles at India-Sindh borders and went on saving Punjab because the military was not only dominated by Punjabis but they considered Punjab to be the core Pakistan. During this, the rulers felt the need of developing security intelligence network and hence, the seeds of today's Inter Services Intelligence (ISI) were sown and for the first time its network was expended to the district level under General Yahya Khan. Unfortunately, the first task to this newly established security outfit was to replace General Ayub Khan. The same network was used to counter Awami League in Bangladesh through Maulana Bhashani; however, Bhashani denied. Since then, the security intelligence organizations in Pakistan are having two major internal security responsibilities – to keep civilians at bay regarding decision-making and to keep non-Punjabi and non-Urdu ethnicities in the outer orbit of state-field.

The world today has given full stop to military rules, therefore Pakistan where army is more developed in comparison with any other institution of society and state has adopted the model of virtual military rule; and has shared its power, legitimacy, and authority to use violence with many non-state civilian actors. Pakistan today is facing the issues of militarization, targeting individuals, and interfering civil and political governance. The possibility to reform state ideology, security doctrine and development paradigm are thin.

(e) Fragile statehood

After undergoing the process of civilly militarized statehood, the state field in Pakistan started facing the internal crisis especially after 9/11. Pakistan's engagement through *Mujahideen* in Afghanistan since 1980s against USSR and later on in Indian Kashmir had started changing its state characteristic through sharing the legitimacy of sate over violence making with many religious groups. During sudden one-eighty degree shift in its regional policy for the strategic use of religious extremists in the aftermath of 9/11, Pakistani establishment was completely rotten and crept-in by the *Islamization*, therefore it cannot de-Islamize the state-field. During the two-decades long interaction between state-field and religious extremists, extremists made inroads into the deeper core of the state; and hence later created pressure groups within the state apparatus, security establishment, civil bureaucracy, government, media and society in general. This aimed to further the Islamist agenda within Pakistan as well as in South-Central Asian region along with the Middle East and East Asia. The liberal, secular, and ethnic nationalists of Pakistan opposed this. In such a situation, the state apparatus in Pakistan in the second decade of twenty first century have not only become civilly militarized but also a fragile-statehood as well.

Disorder and ethnography of state

Pakistani federalism has some peculiarities along with inbuilt permanent features. It is running eight systems in one country in order to protect the interests of Punjabi-Urdu dominated military establishment at the cost of others.

Sindh and Punjab provinces are almost modern democracies. Balochistan is a tribal-cum-democratic administration. KP adopts two administrative systems in which major cities of Indus river plains are modern democracies; meanwhile rest is the Federal Criminal Regulation Area (FCR or semi tribal areas). Federally Administered Tribal Areas (FATA), adjacent to KP is historically and ethno-linguistically part of KP, however dealt as an autonomous tribal administrative system albeit supervised by the Governor of KP, although KP Government has no constitutional say in the FATA affairs. On the other hand, Shariat Law is also adopted in some parts of tribal areas. [34]

Since the birth of the country, Sindhi, Baloch, and Pashtun were considered security threats by the Punjabi-Muhajir civil-military leadership therefore, they were excluded from the state building process. In 1946, Sindhis and Pashtuns were against the idea of Pakistan. As a result, KP Provincial Legislative Assembly was dismissed in September 1947. Sindh Assembly was dismissed in April 1948 due to their refusal for separating Karachi from Sindh in order to establish the Pakistani capital there and resisting Urdu speaking refugee's violence against the Sindhi Hindu.

The "independent, autonomous, and sovereign States [countries]" of undivided India as mentioned in the 1940 Resolution of Pakistan, were basically independent countries before the British invasion, however after creation of Pakistan in 1947 they were downgraded to the status of provinces against the communiqué of 1940 Resolution.[35] Later on, in 1951, the status of provinces was again undone and a unitary province of West Pakistan was created countering the demographic majority of

Bengalis of East Pakistan. Sindhi and Bengali languages were banned for the academic and official purpose including education, writing, publishing, and printing. Pakistan adopted a unitary political system in the name of 'parity federalism' under the first military rule of General Ayub Khan, which ultimately meant to keep Bengalis out of power, despite the fact that they formed ethno-demographic majority in Pakistan. This was done to secure the interests of Punjabis that were majority in the West Pakistan.[36] This finally led Pakistan to break up in 1971 under military rule of General Yahya Khan.

The remaining Pakistan adopted a new constitution, which turned the country into a virtual unitary system based on the democratic monopoly of the ethnic majority of Punjabis. Today, Sindh, Balochistan and KP provinces together do not form a constitutionally required two-third majority in the federal legislature, therefore hey cannot jointly legislate against the vast share of the Punjab in the federal parliament.[37] Since the beginning of the country, "ethnically exclusive civil and military bureaucracy devises the foreign policy. Against the constitutional share, the number of Ministry of Foreign Affairs employees and cadres consisting extensively thin share of ethnic Sindhi and Baloch.[38]"

Bhutto was executed under general Zia's martial law imposed in 1977, which led Sindh into a decade-long resistance that was countered through a five-pronged strategy of militarization; criminalization through dacoits; creating tribal fiefdoms in non-tribal Sindh districts; encouraging ethnic violence by *Muhajirs* in Karachi and Hyderabad; and managing demographic influx of Afghan refugees and Punjabis towards Sindh. At one stage during this process, the military was transformed into a separate interest group, and the political process of 1990's in Pakistan was marked by the conflict between civilian and non-civilian actors. [39]

The post 9/11 "Pakistani federalism attempts a viable statehood", however superficially. The decades old, freedom movements in Sindh and Balochistan are getting strengthened everyday with ever increasing public sympathies. In Sindh, it became phenomenal on December 27, 2007 in the wake of the assassination of Benazir Bhutto, when Pakistan ceased to exist in Sindh for three days as the violent reaction by the people halted the movement of security agencies and government officials[40]. Since then the freedom movement in Sindh has become a popular demand, on the margins of which hundreds of thousands took to the streets of Karachi as well as across the Sindh on Jeay Sindh Qomi Mahaz (JSQM) in 2009[41] and later on in 2012[42]. If analyzed boldly, Pakistani federalism is nothing but a demographic colonialism of ethnic Punjabis and their allies over the rest.

Oligarchy of Interest Transformation
The state apparatus became overdeveloped in comparison with society especially by the end of eighties and was civilly militarized during nineties. "The groups acting on the state field used their position to create a new capitalist dynamic and even a capitalist class, which became their ally."[43] The bureaucrats used their position to their own profit. They built up ties to the emergent capitalist class and to the landed aristocracy. "This attempt to develop a viable economy and a stable political framework failed, since it was against the popular sentiment, particularly in East Pakistan."[44] The army gradually gained a very prominent role in the economy by controlling vital parts of the economic flows within and outside the state.

The upside down change in the state characteristic started taking place in mid seventies during Prime Minister Z. A. Bhutto's period. Boris Wilke[45] writes that when they handed over the rest state to the civilian actors, the generals could count on constitutional and non-constitutional safeguards guaranteeing access to the commanding heights in case of emergency. Besides, they monopolized the key foreign policy issues and kept the control over the military budget. The civilian governments worked under tutelage of the army... Although the military as a corporate actor also made its bargain, it had to rely on state income.

The process of characteristic change of the state has "turn(ed) into downsizing or redeployment of the state."[46] However, in order to curtail the share of military expenditures, "the army would have to transform itself at least partially into a civilian actor." "Given the army's history as guardian of the state, it should be of no surprise that they are in charge of redeploying Pakistan. Success, however, is not guaranteed, and 'anti-state' forces are waiting." [47]The crisis Pakistan is facing today in the form of democratic sustenance and governance is essentially a crisis of the state.

A failure beyond the geopolitics
 Given geo-political importance, versatile geographical texture, and extraordinary reservoirs of natural resources, Pakistan was supposed to be "an extraordinary state". There was a strong perception around the globe in past that "Pakistan is too big and potentially too dangerous for the international community to allow it simply to fail;"[48] however the perception is gradually changing these days.

Many a perceptions prevail today regarding Pakistan in the concerned world that include a 'rogue' or 'terrorist' state; or according to the revised terminology of the U. S. Department of State, a 'state of concern'. According to some writers, it may be more accurate to describe Pakistan as a "persistently failing state" – "one that has continued to exhibit major signs of failure but has not fully collapsed"[49]. Stephan P. Cohen[50] writes that Pakistan's unique feature is not its potential as a failed state (alone) but the intricate interaction between the physical/political/legal entity known as the state of Pakistan and the idea of the Pakistani nation.

Before 9/11, a large number of analysts and observers believed that Pakistan was on the verge of collapse. When the military seized power in late 1999, it was concluded that the state had failed and its economy was to collapse, and "its core institutions were in crises". It initiated a war with India in 1999 over Kargil, which invited a huge international pressure on Pakistan, isolating it diplomatically, resulting into the withdrawal of forces from Kargil and paying a greater setback to Pakistan's Kashmir policy. The winds of narrative change blew suddenly in the post 9/11 scenario, when the west opined that Pakistan was not likely to "experience a breakaway ethnic-group situation similar to the East Pakistan/ Bengali movement of 1970 anytime soon."[51]

Stephan P. Cohen[52] describes Pakistan as a state seemingly incapable of establishing a normal political system, supporting the radical Islamic Taliban, and mounting *Jihadi* operations into India, while its own economy and political system were collapsing and internal religious and ethnic-based violence were rising dramatically.

The military coup by General Pervez Musharraf despite being unwelcomed locally and internationally at initial stages was considered as a corridor of hope later on due to his posture for transforming Pakistan into liberal, secular, and democratic state. Expectations rose that he would be able to convert the state apparatus from religious extremism to the liberal and moderate, and thereby, minimize the possibilities of state failure in Pakistan. Contrarily, the expectations could not materialize; the international interests were shoved in the abyss that was often considered as a 'deceptive positivity' betraying the interests of international allies of Pakistan in the war on terrorism.

Realizing Pakistan's new geo-strategic importance in the context of war on terrorism and concern that "a failing Pakistan could pose a threat to the international community"[53], US collaborated with Pakistan and issued aid of millions of US dollars for the strengthening of state institutions as well as broader civil domain. Pakistan's failure in the war against terror in the ethnic Pashtun FATA, KP and rest of the country has been a reason behind a widening trust deficit questioning its commitment in the war on terrorism.

Besides, the rising concerns over the existence of Taliban hard core in Pakistan, their violent involvement in the Afghanistan along with syndicate with other Islamist outfits of South Asia have been instrumental to question the Pakistani intentions and commitment regarding de-Talibanizing the region. It seems that internalizations of religious extremism by the state apparatus in Pakistan have raised questions by the international community regarding the Pakistan's intention as well as commitment in the war on terrorism. This did not only widen the trust deficit and coordination gap between Pakistan and ISAF on Paki-Afghan borders, but also led to a higher degree of antagonism at various stages.

The failure of Pakistan inside its own territory and in the South Asia is mostly due to its decisive security establishment; however, it has proven drawbacks in the foreign policy making. "Pakistan's foreign policy and strategic vision consists of two basic interconnected factors – inward external security and outward internal concerns .defined within the context of its relationship with Afghanistan and India."[54] Today, the strategic foundations of Pakistan's foreign policies have shifted from USA to Saudi Kingdom and China. Pakistan in last two decades has been facilitating retrogressive Arab nationalism in its proxy war being fought in Afghanistan in the form of Taliban and Al-Qaida. Pakistan aspires a pro-Pakistan Pashtun government in Afghanistan, if Taliban, the globally acknowledged 'strategic assets of Pakistan, become unable to take hold of the country after ISAF withdrawal in 2014.[55]

Punjab has been the beneficial most of the Afghanistan engagement. On the contrary, KP, Sindh, and Balochistan have paid the price for that in the form of the influx of refugees, *Talibanization* and terrorism. "Sindh, the only secular province of Pakistan, is now also facing the possibility of being *Talbanized* as the lethal International Security Assistance Forces (ISAF) supply as well as Afghanistan bound trade is being carried through Karachi, the capital of Sindh. Unfortunately, the international community that is engaged in the reconstruction of Afghanistan has never pressurized Pakistan to ensure the federal rights of Sindh province."[56]

Pakistan's failure has been temporarily halted by "the resisting the downward trends in the state failure indicators"[57]; however, the permanent aversion of failure can only be attained through major transformation and reforms in the statecraft, federal structure and governance framework along with economic revitalization. "In the long run, however, the lack of economic opportunity, the booming birth rate, and the weak educational system could leave Pakistan with a large, young, and poorly educated population that has few prospects for economic advancement."[58] Pakistan, at this stage, does not seem to intent carrying drastic reforms in the state chemistry mostly due to Punjabi interests.

The failure of Pakistan is feared to be a "multidimensional geo-strategic calamity"[59], generating enormous uncertainties in the world. Concerns like a collapsing Pakistan would immediately place risks for Iran, India, and China that includes risk of migrations, eruptions of violence and strategic concerns. The world fears that the worst would be the possible access of non-state actors or the rogue elements to the nuclear weapons and other means of mass destruction.

If seen otherwise, a wider scope of Pakistan's break-up could also be foreseen in the form of quarantining religious extremism and terrorism, enabling secure access of the international community to Afghanistan and Central Asia, sustenance secular Sindh and Balochistan; securing borders of India and Iran, non-infiltration in Afghanistan and China. It would possibly help developing stable Afghanistan as well as positively change the strategic environment of Arabian Sea.

Mapping the possibilities
The state field in Pakistan is undergoing fourfold crisis that ultimately challenges the very sustainable existence of the country.

(a) Ethnic-nationalism
Pakistan has never attempted cementing the various provincial ethnicities in the process of nation building; therefore, ethnic-nationalism started emerging during the first decade after creation of Pakistan. Sindhi, Baloch, Pashtun and Bengali ethnic-nationalism was dominating Pakistan before 1971. After freedom of Bangladesh, Sindhi and Baloch nationalism has been the centre stage of Pakistani socio-political momentum; however Pashtun nationalism hitherto has remained accommodative. During early 1980s, Siraiki ethnic-nationalist movement in South Punjab and Bilawar ethnic-nationalism in Gilgit-Baltistan also emerged, however in relatively weaker form. The ethnic nationalist movements in Pakistan in their essence are against the hegemony of Punjab and are secular in their political ideologies and culture.

The ethnic nationalist movements in Sindh and Balochistan were of similar nature in their issues and demands. Both were and are having the differences with the federation as well as the province of Punjab on the water rights, natural resources exploitation, share in the employment opportunities, fiscal and financial share proportionate to their contribution in the federal revenue, GDP, social, human and physical infrastructure and development disparities. The Siraiki ethnic-nationalist movement is because of development disparities between northern Punjab Siraiki speaking South Punjab in association with the issue of historical identity of Siraikis.

The ethnic-nationalist movements these days dominate political scene in Pakistan. Baloch are waging war against Pakistan Army since more than a decade, in which hundreds from both side have been killed so far and thousands of Baloch have been involutedly abducted by the security agencies. Sindhi movement has various outlooks. The stronger most is the peaceful mass movement for the freedom of Sindh in which around one million Sindhis gathered in Karachi on March 23, 2013[60] demanding separate sovereign state of Sindhis and sought world powers intervention for the freedom of their homeland. Earlier, on November 7, 2009[61] around half a million Sindhi gathered in Karachi, demanding the sovereign status of Sindh of pre- British occupation of 1843. Hundreds of Sindhi activists have been killed by the security agencies in last three decades as well as dozens of military personnel were also killed during the low-scale insurgency since 1983. A large number of tortured and bullet ridden dead bodies of Baloch and Sindhi activist have been found on the roadside in the various towns and cities of Sindh and Balochistan, for which military is generally held responsible.

The real picture is eye opening. The rite of Pakistan government in Balochistan is limited to Quetta city only. The students across the Balochi speaking Balochistan primary and higher secondary schools hoist the flag of independent Balochistan and reciting the liberationists' Balochistan national anthem. Unlike Balochistan, Sindh is moving with the popular movement for freedom, with low scale insurgency. On December 27[62], after the murder of ex-prime minister Benazir Bhutto in Punjab, Sindhi activists took hold of everything of the province and started guarding Sindh-Punjab provincial borders; however they were dispersed only when Asif Zardari (husband of Benazir Bhutto) appealed them to not declare independence.

There is a violent movement of lingual Urdu refugees. Their politics until now has been in collaboration with the dominant ethnic Punjabis to acquire more socio-economic and political share from Sindh province although being a minority consisting 19 percent[63] population in the province. Mutahida Qomi Movement (MQM) claims to be their political representative, which was established in the military regime of General Zia against Sindhi insurgency in 1980s.

(b) Extremism and violence

The increasing extremism in Pakistan has deep roots in the state-field of the country. The state of Pakistan since 1980s has started sharing its legitimate authority to use violence for war or peace making with the non-state paramilitary groups -- all of them have been the Islamic extremists excepting MQM.[64]

The sharing the legitimate authority over use of violence with religious outfits was meant to defeat Soviet Union in Afghanistan, unease India in Kashmir and reduce influence of Iran through victimizing Shiites of Pakistan; however MQM was supported to counter the freedom movement by Sindhis, which Pakistani establishment still considered a greater internal security challenge. Similar pattern was adopted in Balochistan by socio-economically strengthening Persian-speaking Hazara refugees from Afghanistan and in Khyber Pakhtunkhuwa province by supporting Hindko speaking community of Hazara Division.

In the post 9/11 scene, the religious militant groups were playing a role given to them by their real masters playing "dual role" in the war on terrorism. Today, South Punjab, FATA, and some parts of Pashtun belt in

Balochistan have become Taliban strongholds in which central Punjab is playing a role of nursery to nurture them. [65] Sindh is the only remaining secular province of Pakistan where religious outfits are trying to Talbanise it through increasing numbers of their *Madersas* and enhancing their political presence; however, it would genuinely be difficult for them to control Sindh and convert it into a Taliban region.

(c) Fragility of society

The exclusion from the state field, centralized federal system, and continuous economic exploitation by the Punjabi dominated establishment has further fragmentized Pakistan on the ethnic lines, which seems to be deepen on the line of stronger and most probably popular and violent ethnic nationalism in Sindh and Balochistan.

(d) Chaos and anarchy

Pakistan is inching toward directionless ends, where the antagonism along with lack of coordination between various schools of thought within the state fold as well as society has been giving space to the upcoming anarchy. The phenomenon has created a chaotic environment where Pakistani state has lost vitality, adaptability, and dynamics to reform itself and is in indecisive mode to redirect internal security relations with the external as well as country's broader security doctrine. It has furthered the state failure indicators.

Speculating Future

"When security, human services, justice, and basic necessities are not provided to the population, states fail. The case of Pakistan, however, is different as well as more difficult."[66] The ongoing anarchy in Pakistan has opened up a new Pandora box of various failures within the state and society. The anarchy of democratic institutions and modern legal system has already lost its legitimacy turning Pakistan into an operative mode of state governance; therefore, two scenarios have strongly emerged in the light of Rodney W Jones's[67] report:

> (i)   The socio-economic chaos due economic and development failure in the face of extensive population growth is leading Pakistan towards collapse, which is bound to cause a greater humanitarian crisis like ethnic and sub-ethnic strife as well as out-migrations;

> (ii)   The state order has started compromising and possibly subdue to the warlords, fiefdoms, mafias, and violent Islamist groups having extensive penetration in state institutions particularly in the military and security agencies. Therefore, a kind of turf war has emerged internally over capturing maximum power as well as economic assets. This also hints at the possibilities for the forces of anarchy that already have inroad into security institutions may lead to the factional contest for control over the strategic assets.

The situation may lead to new changes in Pakistan by the end of second half of ongoing decade possibly on the bellow lines:

> (i)   The civil wars and breakup of Pakistan into independent states on the ethno-linguistic lines;

> (ii)   The security establishment may eventually choose an Iranian–cum-Saudi model of statehood to avert failure;

> (iii)   A state of extensive disorder may continue for a relatively longer period giving space to further fragmentation of Pakistan society.

The state failure in Pakistan is already underway. Pakistani establishment has only one option of avoiding collapse through extensive as well as judicious reforms based on geographic, ethno-demographic, economic, and cultural sovereignties of the provinces into countryhood in accordance with AIML's 1940 Resolution as well as Sindh Assembly Resolution of 1943. It essentially requires their proportionate share in the civil and military components of state-field as well as proportionate participation to development according to their economic contribution in the federation. Ending military-mullah nexus, and separating religion from the state affairs besides necessary structural and recruitment process changes in the Pakistan Army's ethnic, and its sectarian, religious and gender composition would be the foundation of creation of new EU like Pakistan if UN membership of the countries that are called Provinces in Pakistan has to be a distant.

The time has come for the nations or ethnicities in Pakistan to be ready for possible adversaries hidden in the future. If there is re-structuring and re-construction of Pakistani state on the above lines (that are unlikely to happen), they should take active part in giving shapes to the political and economic frameworks and other dispositions. In case of anarchy, they should be ready to protect their land, population, assets, and integrity and uphold secular and liberal value.

International and regional insecurity
The migrant, overdeveloped and garrison forms of statehood in Pakistan has already proved to be disastrous for not only 180 million people of Pakistan especially for Sindhi, Baloch and Pashtun but also regionally for Afghanistan and India and internationally for USA, UK and EU out of which later have strategic interests in the Central-South Asia. It has also challenged the interests of the Central Asian Countries like Tajikistan that is landlocked and have only nearest hot water excess from Karachi

Port through Afghanistan as well as Port Abaas in Iran via Afghanistan. A fragile or civilly militarized state in Pakistan has further challenged their interests. It will further pose security and strategic risks to the all nations bordering Pakistan and create an un-conducive environment for the West that wants a meaningful intervention in Central Asia through Afghanistan.

In such a grave situation, Pakistan's journey towards anarchy after fragility would be the worst most as well as its conversion into a theocratic dictatorship like Iran-cum-Saudi model would be leaving far reaching negative strategic impacts on the region and the global politics. The only two options are more comprehendible for the all stakeholders: a state chemistry change in Pakistan through proportionate share of excluded ethnicities like Sindhi, Baloch, Pashtun and Siraikis into the state-field particularly in the security establishment or creation of new sovereign states out of debris of failing Pakistan. The earlier is almost impossible at this juncture of time as it have crossed the limits of irreversibility; however the later needs to be more planned to avoid any major disaster.

In such a grave situation, Pakistan's journey towards anarchy after fragility would be the worst most as well as its conversion into a theocratic dictatorship like Iran-cum-Saudi system would be leaving far reaching negative strategic impacts on the region and the global politics. There is only comprehensible option for the all stakeholders: a state chemistry change in Pakistan through proportionate share of excluded nations (ethnicities) like Sindhi, Baloch, Pashtun and Siraikis into the state-field particularly in the security establishment along with creation of new sovereign "States" (countries) in accordance with the 1940 and 1943 historical resolutions for the countryhood of the lands in Pakistan that were invaded by the Britain in 19th century while these were independent and sovereign countries.

References

[1] Jackson, H. Robert, Quasi States: Sovereignty, International Relations, and the Third World, Cambridge, UK, 1990

[2] Commission on the Weak States and US National Security, On the Brinks: Weak States and US National Security – CBD, Washington, USA, 2003

[3] Wilke, Boris, State Formation and the Military in Pakistan, Universitat Hamburg – IPW, Germany, 2001

[4] Ibid

[5] Jaffrelot, Christoph (Ed.), A History of Pakistan and Its Origins, Anthem Press, 2005

[6] Shah, Zulfiqar, The Centre cannot hold, *Daily Kathmandu Post*, Nepal, May 01, 2013

[7] Shah, Zulfiqar, Federalism in Pakistan: Important Lessons, *Daily Republica, Kathmandu*, Nepal, June 28, 2012

[8] Alavi, Hamza, Authoritarianism and legitimating of state power in Pakistan, in: *Mitra, Subrata Kumar et al (ed.), The Post-Colonial State in Asia. Dialectics of Politics and Culture, New York 1990,* pp.19-7 1

[9] Migdal, S. Joel, Strong Societies, and Weak States: State-Society Relations and State Capabilities in the Third World, Princeton, USA, 1988

[10] Mitropolitski, Simeon, Weber's Definition of the State as an Ethnographic Tool for Understanding the Contemporary Political Science State of the Discipline – SSRN, USA, 2011

[11] Dolek, Caglar, Pakistan in Crisis: a State Failure or Unequal Power Constructs? *Turkish Weekly*, Anqara, Turkey, January 29, 2008,

[12] Wilke, *Op. Cit.* 2001

[13] Wilke, *Op. Cit.* 2001

[14] Wilke, *Op. Cit.* 2001

[15] Wilke, *Op. Cit.* 2001

[16] Wilke, *Op. Cit.* 2001

[17] Alavi, Hamza 1998, Pakistan-US Military Alliance, in *Economic and Political Weekly*, Bombay, August 20, 1998

[18] Wilke, *Op. Cit.* 2001

[19] Wilke, *Op. Cit.* 2001

[20] Ansari, Sara, Life after Partition: Migration, Community and Strife in Sindh, 1947-1962, OUP, 2005, p.255

[21] Ibid

[22] Ibid

[23] Syed, GM, The Case of Sindh, Naeen Sindh Academy, Karachi, 1994

[24] Wilke, *Op. Cit.* 2001

[25] Alavi, *Op. Cit.* 1998

[26] Jalal, Ayesha, The State of Martial Rule. The Origins of Pakistan's Political Economy of Defense, Cambridge, UK, 1990

[27] Ibid

[28] Wilke, *Op. Cit.* 2001

[29] Wilke, *Op. Cit.* 2001

[30] Shah, *Op. Cit.* 2013

[31] Shah, Zulfiqar, Can civilians win the war in Pakistan, Asia Times, Hong Kong, August 30, 2012

[32] Ibid

[33] Ibid

[34] Shah, Zulfiqar, Federalism in Pakistan: Important Lessons, *Daily Republica, Kathmandu*, Nepal, June 28, 2012

[35] Shah, Zulfiqar, The Centre cannot hold, Daily Kathmandu Post, Nepal, May 01, 2013

[36] Shah, *Op. Cit.* 2012

[37] Shah, *Op. Cit.* 2013

[38] Shah, Zulfiqar, Pakistan: What does future hold? *The Descrier, UK*, August 27, 2013

[39] Shah, *Op. Cit.* 2012

[40] Shah, Zulfiqar, Roots of Nationalism in Sindh, *Encounter, Daily Dawn*, Karachi, 2007

[41] Daily The News, Karachi (Islamabad Edition), JSQM's Azadi March demands pre-1843 status, November 8, 2009, (front page), Islamabad, Karachi

[42] Daily Express Tribune, (Karachi Edition) Pakistan Day: JSQM leader demands freedom for Sindh and Balochistan, March 24, 2012, http://tribune.com.pk/story/354308/pakistan-day-jsqm-leader-demands-freedom-for-sindh-and-balochistan/

[43] Wilke, *Op. Cit.* 2001

[44] Wilke, Op. Cit. 2001

[45] Wilke, *Op. Cit.* 2001

[46] Rashid, Ahmed Taliban. Islam, Oil and the New Great Game in Central Asia, London – New York, 1999

[47] Wilke, *Op. Cit.* 2001

[48] Cohen, P. Stephen, The Nation and the State in Pakistan in *The Washington Quarterly*, 25(3), pp.109-122, 2002

[49] Ibid

[50] Ibid

[51] Ibid

[52] Ibid

[53] Ibid

[54] Shah, *Op. Cit.* August 27, 2013

[55] Shah, *Op. Cit.* August 27, 2013

[56] Shah, *Op. Cit.* August 27, 2013

[57] Cohen, *Op. Cit.* 2002

[58] Cohen, *Op. Cit.* 2002

[59] Jones, Rodney W. 2001, The Prospects for State Failure in Pakistan: Ethnic, Regional, and Sectarian Fissures, Summary, Policy Architects International, USA

[60] Daily Express Tribune, (Karachi Edition) Pakistan Day: JSQM leader demands freedom for Sindh and Balochistan, March 24, 2012, http://tribune.com.pk/story/354308/pakistan-day-jsqm-leader-demands-freedom-for-sindh-and-balochistan/

[61] Daily The News, Karachi (Islamabad Edition), JSQM's Azadi March demands pre-1843 status, November 8, 2009, (front page), Islamabad, Karachi

[62] Opednews.com, Benazir's assassination: History is repeating itself by Abdul Sattar Ghazali, December 29, 2007, http://www.opednews.com/articles/genera_abdus_sa_071228_benazir_s_assassinat.htm

[63] Government of Pakistan, Census Report 1998, BoS, Islamabad, Pakistan, 1998
[64] Hoodbhoy, Nafisa, Aboard the Democracy Train, Washington, USA, 2011, pp 41-4
[65] Shah, Zulfiqar, Pakistan Divided over Afghanistan, Daily Outlook Afghanistan, Kabul, Afghanistan, August 13, 2012
[66] Cohen, *Op. Cit.* 2002
[67] Jones, Rodney W. 2001, The Prospects for State Failure in Pakistan: Ethnic, Regional, and Sectarian Fissures, Summary, Policy Architects International, USA

Other Sources

Books

W. Napier, Ed. The Life and Opinions of General Sir C.J.Napier, London
H.T. Lambrick, The Terrorist, Oxford University Press, Karachi, 1995
Cox, Admen, Police and Crime in India, New Delhi, 1910.
Aftab Nabi, The Court Martial, Veer Publication, Karachi, 2002
Dr. S.D.F. Ansari, The Pirs of Sindh, 1937.
Dr. S.D.F. Ansari, Sufi Saints of Sindh and State Powers, 1947
Jotwani, Motilal, Modern Sindh Literature, in K.M. George, Modern Indian Literature: An Anthology, Surveys & Poems, Sahitya Acadmi, India, 1992
Malkani, K. R. The Sindh Story, Sahtiya Akadmi, Delhi 2nd edition, 1997
Mohammad Usman Diplai, Saghar, [Novel], New Fields Publication, 1999 3rd edition.
Prof.Dr.Laiq Ahmed Zaradari, Nawabshah, Nawabshah, 1995.
Panhwar, M. H. Inevitability of the conquest of Sindh by British in 1843 on http://panhwar.com/Article07.htm , accessed on June 25, 2013
Panhwar, M. H. The Economic Plight of Sindh Under Pakistan, Sindh Quarterly, Vol. 18, 1990
Syed, G. M., The Case of Sindh, Naeen Sindh Academy, Karachi, November 1994
Sindhi, Dada, Sindhian Ji Fauji Maharat (Expertise of Sindhis in Art of War), Hyderabad 1988

Journals & Magazines

Quarterly Jhungar, Sanghar (2000-2002) available at Central Library, University of Sindh, Jamshoro, Pakistan
Quarterly Mansoor Sanghar [2000-2002] available at Central Library, University of Sindh, Jamshoro, Pakistan
Sindh Quarterly, Karachi (1982) available at Central Library, University of Sindh, Jamshoro, Pakistan

Newspapers

Daily Azad, Karachi. [1942-1944] available at Sind Achieve Library, Culture Department, Govt. of Sindh, Karachi
Daily Bombay Chronicle, Bombay [1942-43] available at Sind Achieve Library, Culture Department, Govt. of Sindh, KarachiIbrat
Daily Ibrat, Hyderabad, (1965 – 2012)

Daily Kawish, Hyderabad, (1995 – 2012)
Daily Awami Awaz, Hyderabad, (1990 – 2012)
Daily Dawn, Karachi, (1995 – 2012)

Websites : www.merinews.com